paperblanks®
BLUE VELVET

Notre modèle Velours Bleu s'inspire d'une pièce de dalmatique en velours du XVème siècle. Celle-ci porte les motifs d'un bouclier à sept lobes contenant une forme botanique similaire à un artichaut et orné de petits motifs floraux sur chaque côté. Le motif a été créé avec du fil de métal doré, un processus à la fois onéreux et fastidieux, faisant ainsi du velours l'un des tissus de luxe les plus prisés de la Renaissance.

Unser Motiv Samtblau geht auf eine Samtdalmatik aus dem 15. Jahrhundert zurück. Sie ist mit einem siebenbogigen Wappen verziert, das ein botanisches Symbol in Form einer Artischocke enthält, die auf jeder Seite mit winzigen Blumenmustern versehen ist. Für das Muster wurde der Stoff mit einem Goldfaden durchwirkt – ein teures und mühsames Verfahren, wodurch Samtstoffe wie dieser zu den kostbarsten Luxusgeweben der Renaissance zählten.

Il nostro design Velluto Blu s'ispira a una dalmatica di velluto del XV secolo. Il disegno riproduce uno scudo a sette lobi con una forma botanica all'interno che ricorda un carciofo, impreziosito da piccoli fiori. Il design originale è stato creato usando filo metallico dorato e applicando una costosa e minuziosa tecnica, usata nel Rinascimento per trasformare tessuti di velluto di questo tipo in preziosi e lussuosi capolavori.

Nuestro diseño Terciopelo Azul está inspirado en una dalmática de terciopelo del siglo XV, decorada con un brocado de hilo dorado que reproduce un motivo repetido de arco de siete lóbulos. En su interior destaca un elemento vegetal en forma de alcachofa con florecillas a cada lado. Por el elevado coste y complejidad de su proceso de elaboración, el terciopelo era uno de los tejidos más suntuosos y apreciados del Renacimiento.

本装丁は、15世紀に作られたベルベット地のダルマティカ（カトリックの司祭服）にインスピレーションを得て生まれました。七つの切れ目の入った盾の中に、チョウセンアザミのような植物のパターンが配され、両側には小さな花の模様があしらわれています。これらの模様はすべて金糸刺繍によるものです。たいへんな手間と費用のかかる手作業によって、このようなルネッサンス期の貴重なベルベット生地が生み出されることとなりました。

BLUE VELVET

Blue Velvet

Our Blue Velvet design is inspired by a piece of a fifteenth-century velvet dalmatic. The original panel was given to the Metropolitan Museum of Art as part of the Rogers Fund in 1945. It is patterned with a seven-lobed shield that contains an artichoke-like botanical shape adorned with tiny floral patterns on each side. The patterning was created using brocaded gilt metal thread.

Velvets were originally woven on a special loom that created two thicknesses at the same time in order to achieve their marvellously soft texture. It was an expensive and painstaking procedure, making velvets like this some of the most highly prized luxury fabrics of the Renaissance.

ISBN: 978-1-4397-6388-9
SLIM FORMAT 176 PAGES LINED
DESIGNED IN CANADA

Image copyright © The Metropolitan Museum of Art
Image source: Art Resource, NY
Printed on acid-free sustainable forest paper.
© 2018 Hartley & Marks Publishers Inc. All rights reserved.
No part of this book may be reproduced without written permission from the publisher. Paperblanks are published by
Hartley & Marks Publishers Inc. and
Hartley & Marks Publishers Ltd. Made in China.
North America 1-800-277-5887
Europe 800-3333-8005
Japan 0120-177-153

paperblanks.com